A RAILWAY LINE IN TAKANAWA

The impact of modernisation was being felt around the world. One of the biggest changes was the advance of the railways whose lines were spreading like tentacles across the countryside, linking cities and even countries. It was possible for the ordinary person to be mobile, to work in one place and live in another, hastening the speed of social change. In Japan the abolition of the Shoguns signalled a new era, one which was to modernise a country whose borders had until recently been closed to the rest of the world.

THE PARIS COMMUNE IN 1871

After the elections in France in February 1871 a revolutionary Republican commune was set up in Paris in opposition to the government in Versailles. The French army was sent in to recapture Paris and in the bloody street fighting that followed more than 20,000 died.

THE WORLD OF MONET

THE NOUVELLE ATHENES CAFE

Cafe society was very important to the artist community in Paris. It was in the cafes that they sat and talked, exchanged ideas, and often painted pictures. The Nouvelle Athenes Cafe became a meeting ground for the Impressionists.

Oscar Claude Monet was born on 14 November 1840 at Rue Lafitte, Paris, the son of a grocer. When he was very young the family moved to Le Havre on the coast in order that Monet's father could join the family wholesale business. Monet's mother died when he was just 17 years old. The only early indication of his artistic leanings were his caricatures which he sold for 10 or 20 francs each. A local artist named Eugene Boudin saw Monet's caricatures displayed in an artist's materials shop and encouraged Monet to paint. Boudin took Monet on painting excursions into the countryside. This *plein air* (open air) method of oil painting was extremely unusual for the time. Monet said *'The fact that I've become a painter I owe to Boudin... I announced to my father that I wanted to become a painter and went off to Paris to study art'.*

THE BEACH AT TROUVILLE *Eugene Boudin*

Boudin was a very influential figure in Monet's life. He met Boudin shortly after the death of his mother, and Boudin taught Monet to paint out of doors directly in front of the subject. Boudin is reported to have told Monet that *'everything that is painted on the spot has a strength, an intensity and a vividness that cannot be recreated in the studio'.*

MONET
IMPRESSIONISM

BY
DAVID SPENCE

THE WORLD IN THE 1870'S

In the United States in 1870 John Rockefeller founded the Standard Oil Company.

*E*urope was changing in the 1870's. On 19 July 1870 Napoleon III of France declared war on Prussia. The Prussian Chancellor, Otto von Bismarck, with the support of all the German states, quickly defeated Napoleon's armies. Napoleon was taken prisoner and the people of Paris suffered a siege which lasted four months during which thousands died of cold and starvation before peace was signed in January 1871. Bismarck united the German states into a formidable new German Empire. This was to prove competition for the dominant British Empire which in 1877 proclaimed Queen Victoria as Empress of all India. At the same time across the Atlantic the country which was to dominate the next 100 years was growing fast. In 1870 the population of the United States was 39 million. Just 30 years later it would stand at 76 million.

CITY LIFE

Photography, still in its infancy, captured the bustling city street life. Paris was the acknowledged art capital of the world but all major cities such as London and New York contained artists' communities. American artists such as James Whistler and Mary Cassatt were attracted to Paris to be close to the centre of the revolution in art.

FRANCO-PRUSSIAN WAR

As a result of the Franco-Prussian war France lost the provinces of Alsace and much of Lorraine. The French were also required to pay an indemnity of 5 billion francs. The repercussions were graver still in Paris where many had died during the siege. The sparks of unrest which followed were quickly to ignite into a civil war raging on the streets of Paris.

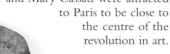

TERRACE AT SAINTE-ADRESSE, 1867

Monet grew up in and around Le Havre on the Normandy coast. Monet's father joined his brother-in-law's business in Le Havre. The family were prosperous and Monet often visited the family's summer house not far from the seaside town of Sainte-Adresse. Monet painted this picture when he returned there in 1867 and included his father, standing on the terrace, in a scene of such freshness that it is almost possible to feel the breeze which whips the flags.

BOULEVARD DES CAPUCINES, 1873

Monet refused to submit to the formal academic school of training when he went to Paris to study. He could not bring himself to concentrate on the studio drawings from life casts and the official Academy view that reality should be sacrificed to the ideal. Monet quickly began to mix with friends who felt the same as he did about art, such as Auguste Renoir and Alfred Sisley. Monet dressed in style despite being hard up. Renoir stated that *'He was penniless, and he wore shirts with lace cuffs'*. His painting of the *Boulevard des Capucines* was made from the studio of photographer 'Nadar'. It is no coincidence that the picture appears similar to an early photograph with movement captured in the blurred figures that rush by in the street below.

Paris must have been an exciting place for the young Monet to live and work, contributing to what art historian E. H. Gombrich has called the 'permanent revolution' in art.

FROZEN IN TIME

The influence of photography was not yet beginning to be felt but the instantaneousness of the photograph, its ability to capture a moment in time, its arbitrary framing of scenes were all qualities that Monet and the other Impressionist painters were seeking in their art.

THE BOATING PARTY LUNCH

Auguste Renoir

Renoir worked with Monet out of doors painting scenes on the river Seine. Monet was to be a strong influence on Renoir, particularly Renoir's use of lighter colours in his paintings. Renoir exhibited at the first three Impressionist exhibitions but eventually his work differed from the Impressionist approach by his use of preparatory drawing and a predetermined colour palette. His efforts to recreate nature using colour resulted in warm and soft pictures, often rose and pink in hue.

ST MARTIN CANAL

Alfred Sisley

Alfred Sisley was of English descent but lived and worked just outside Paris. He devoted himself almost entirely to painting landscapes in the open-air style adopted by the Impressionists. Sisley and Pissarro together with Monet have come to be known as the 'pure' Impressionists, which means that they strived towards naturalism by capturing the fleeting impression of light and its effects, particularly colour and tone, often on the landscape. Sisley went to stay in England during the Franco-Prussian war, painting many scenes from the suburbs surrounding London.

LORDSHIP LANE STATION

Camille Pissarro

Pissarro is the third artist, along with Monet and Sisley, who are considered to be 'pure Impressionist'. Pissarro was born in the West Indies and did not move to Paris until he was 24 years old. He first met Monet in 1859 and his paintings were first exhibited in the *Salon des Refuses* in 1863 and exhibited with the first Impressionist exhibition in 1874. He painted this picture of Lordship Lane Station in the London suburb of Dulwich in 1871. Pissarro lived in London at the time having escaped from the Franco-Prussian war that was tearing Paris apart. It is said that some 200 paintings left behind in his home in France were used by the invading German soldiers as duckboards in the muddy garden.

THE ART OF HIS DAY

Monet became good friends with Frederic Bazille who was studying art in Paris. They shared a studio in the Batignolles quarter of Paris, hence the name given to the Impressionists, the 'Batignolles group'. The aim of all artists, including Monet, was to exhibit work at the Salon. The Salon had existed for over 200 years and was *the* official state gallery, works being selected by the jury of the French Academy of Fine Arts. Its power, however, was fading as the rapidly changing face of art presented new and different works which did not conform to the Academy view. In 1863 a *Salon des Refuses* exhibited paintings that had been rejected by the Jury. This alternative salon was to show more influential paintings than the official Salon but in 1865 Monet had two works accepted by the latter. Edouard Manet came to learn of Monet when the artists' names were confused by the critics. The two artists became friends, learning from each other, Monet persuading Manet to take up open-air painting.

YOUNG WOMAN DRESSED FOR THE BALL

Berthe Morisot

The two best known female Impressionists are Berthe Morisot and Mary Cassatt. Morisot was married to Manet's brother and mixed with the Parisian artist community. She exhibited her paintings at all but one of the Impressionist exhibitions. Women were constrained by social etiquette and it was therefore impossible for them to paint in the open-air manner in the same way as their male counterparts, or deal with the working class subjects covered by the men. Instead what we see in Morisot's work are more domestic interiors and scenes depicting elegant women at leisure.

FAMILY FRIENDS & OTHERS

**TERRACE AT
SAINTE-ADRESSE**

This detail from Monet's painting of 1867 (see page 5) shows Monet's father, Claude Adolphe Monet, standing on the terrace in conversation with a woman holding a yellow parasol, possibly Monet's aunt Madame Lecadre.

The first five years of Monet's life were spent in Paris. His family's move to Le Havre was forced by his father joining brother-in-law Jacques Lecadre's ship chandlery business. Monet's mother died in 1857, when he was seventeen years old. Jacques Lecadre died the following year and his childless widow, Monet's aunt, cared for Monet until he left home a year later. Monet moved to Paris in 1859 to study painting. In 1862 he studied under art tutor Charles Gleyre. It was from 1863 onwards that Monet's circle of friends grew to include some of the most influential artists of the period. He lived in the Batignolles quarter and it was in the Cafe Guerbois in the Rue des Batignolles that he met with fellow artists every Monday night. Monet recollects that '... *Manet invited me to accompany him to a cafe where he and his friends met and talked every evening after leaving their studios. There I met Fantin-Latour, Cezanne and Degas... the art critic Duranty, Emile Zola... I myself took along Bazille and Renoir. Nothing could have been more stimulating than these debates with the constant clashes of opinions'.*

CAMILLE AND JEAN

Monet's first paintings to include Camille Doncieux were made in 1865 when she was nineteen years old. Camille became Monet's mistress and his wife five years later. Their first son, Jean, was born in 1867 and in this double portrait of Camille and Jean' painted in 1873 he would have been about six years old. This picture gave Monet the opportunity to deal with his favourite subject - the effects of light as the sun catches the grass.

STUDIO IN THE BATIGNOLLES QUARTER

Henri Fantin-Latour

Monet first met Bazille at the studio of Charles Gleyre in 1862. Bazille and Monet were to become good friends and in 1865 they shared a studio together at 6 Rue Furstenburg in Paris. Two years later when Monet returned, penniless, to Paris after a stay in Le Havre Bazille again offered a place for Monet to stay. Monet's hopes rested on the exhibition of his large canvas *Women in the Garden* (see page 23) but was not accepted by the Salon and found no buyers from its place of exhibition in the shop window of the artist's supplier Latouche. Bazille bought the painting from Monet, paying for it in instalments. When the Franco-Prussian war began in 1870 Bazille enlisted in the army and tragically was killed by a Prussian sniper at the age of 29. This group portrait shows Manet (seated) painting Astruc's portrait. Behind them are Zola, Maitre, Bazille, Monet, Renoir and Scholderer.

PORTRAIT OF MADAME GAUDIBERT *(detail)*, 1868

One of Monet's first patrons was the shipowner Gaudibert who was based in Le Havre. Gaudibert supported Monet from as early as 1864, but it was four years later that Monet was commissioned to paint this portrait of Madame Gaudibert.

THE LIFE OF MONET

~1840~
Born on 14 November at Rue Lafitte, Paris to Claude Adolphe and Louise Justine Monet

~1845~
Moves with family to Le Havre

~1856~
Starts drawing lessons and meets artist Eugene Boudin

~1857~
Monet's mother dies

~1859~
Decides to go to Paris to study painting where he meets Camille Pissarro

~1861~
Called up for military service and sent to Algeria but falls ill and returns to France

~1865~
Shares studio with Bazille where he meets Cezanne and Manet. Meets Camille Doncieux

~1867~
Birth of son Jean

~1870~
Marries Camille. Outbreak of Franco-Prussian war. Monet travels to London

FAMILY FORTUNES

MONEY FROM SHOPPING

The Hoschede department-store fortune did not last. Ernest Hoschede was declared bankrupt in 1877 forcing him to sell his art collection. Ernest died on 18 March 1891 enabling his widow Alice to resolve the ambiguous relationship between the Hoschede and Monet families. Alice had been Monet's mistress long before they were finally able to be married in 1892. Monet and Alice were together until Alice's death in 1911.

In 1876 after several successful years as an artist, which also included several financial crises, Monet met the department store owner Ernest Hoschede. Hoschede was an admirer of Monet and invited him to the Hoschede estate at the Chateau de Rottenburg where Monet was given his own studio in the park. Monet was commissioned to produce four decorative paintings for the chateau. Camille and Jean stayed at home in Argenteuil while Monet was at the chateau and it may have been during this time, when Monet and Hoschede's wife Alice spent many an evening together, that they became lovers. Certainly their deep friendship started here. Hoschede supported many of the Impressionists; when his business ran into trouble in 1878 he was forced to sell all the paintings, causing prices and therefore the market value of their work to fall.

CAMILLE MONET ON HER DEATHBED, 1879

Monet was driven to paint the tragic scene of his wife on her deathbed. He later said *'I caught myself watching her tragic temples, almost mechanically searching for the changing shades which death imposed upon her rigid face. Blue, yellow, grey, whatever... even before the idea had occurred to me to record her beloved features my organism was already reacting to the sensation of colour...'.*

A POWERFUL FRIEND (detail), Edouard Manet

The French statesman Georges Clemenceau was a staunch supporter of Monet. Clemenceau ran a magazine entitled *La Justice* which carried many favourable reviews of Monet's paintings and even articles written by Clemenceau himself. He was instrumental in acquiring paintings by Monet for the state, especially after 1907 when he became Prime Minister of France. Clemenceau is perhaps best known for his Treaty of Versailles negotiations after the first world war. This portrait was painted by Monet's friend Edouard Manet in 1880.

JEAN MONET ASLEEP, 1868

When Monet's son, Jean, was 12 years old he inherited six more brothers and sisters. The unhappy financial fortunes of the Hoschede family meant they were in need of a home. Ernest Hoschede, his wife Alice and their six children went to live with Claude and Camille Monet, their son Jean and new-born son Michel in a house in the Rue des Mantes in Ventheuil thirty miles outside Paris. Camille was very ill and it soon became clear she was dying. On 5 September 1879, after a long illness, Camille died. After her death Monet's sons Jean and Michel were brought up by Alice Hoschede alongside her own children.

OPEN AIR STUDY - WOMAN TURNED TO THE LEFT

The model for this *plein air* study, made in 1886, is thought to be Monet's step-daughter, Suzanne Hoschede. Suzanne married the American artist Theodore Butler in 1892 but died suddenly in 1899. Monet and Suzanne's mother Alice were deeply affected by her death.

THE LIFE OF MONET

~1871~
His father dies.
Monet travels to Holland.
He receives support
from dealer Paul
Durand-Ruel

~1874~
First group
Impressionist exhibition

~1876~
Becomes friends with
Alice and Ernest Hoschede.
Camille falls ill

~1878~
Second son Michel
is born

~1879~
Camille dies.
Fourth Impressionism
exhibition held

~1880~
Monet's first one man
exhibition is a success

~1887~
Monet's paintings
exhibited in New York
by Durand-Ruel

~1889~
A record price of 10,000
francs paid for a
Monet painting

~1892~
Marries Alice Hoschede

~1893~
Buys land at Giverny to
develop water garden

~1911~
Alice Hoschede dies

~1912~
Doctors diagnose cataracts
in both of Monet's eyes

SUCCESS

onet became famous in his own lifetime. The early years were a struggle with money in short supply but eventually he found patrons willing to support him. It is true to say that life was never as hard for Monet as it was for some artists, Vincent van Gogh for example, but his commitment to his art was absolute. Monet was enjoying a degree of success while in his forties and by the time he was in his fifties his recognition was such that American artists went to Giverny to be near him, resulting in one, Theodore Butler, actually marrying into the Monet family. As a result of this widespread recognition there exist today many records of interviews with Monet as well as articles, reviews and family memoirs.

MADAME CLAUDE MONET WITH HER SON JEAN IN THE GARDEN AT ARGENTEUIL

Auguste Renoir

One of Monet's recollections described a visit by Manet in 1874 when Auguste Renoir was staying with Monet at Argenteuil. Monet's wife Camille and son Jean were sitting in the garden. All three artists set up their easels to paint the scene. *'One day, excited by the colours and light, Manet started an open air study of figures under trees. While he was working, Renoir came along. He too was captured by the mood of the moment. He asked me for palette, brush and canvas, sat down next to Manet and started painting. Manet watched him out of the corner of his eye and now and again went over to look at his canvas... he tiptoed over to me and whispered 'The lad has no talent. Since you are his friend tell him he might as well give up.'*

THE GARE SAINT-LAZARE

Monet knew the Gare Saint-Lazare well as it was from here that he took the train to both Argenteuil and Le Havre. In 1877 Monet exhibited seven views of the station along with other works in a show of group Impressionist works. The story of how Monet came to paint these pictures is recounted by Jean Renoir. *'One day he said 'I've got it! The Gare Saint-Lazare' I'll show it just as the trains are starting, with smoke from the engines so thick you can hardly see a thing. It's a fascinating sight, a dream world.'* He did not of course intend to paint it from memory. He would paint it *in situ* so as to capture the play of sunlight on the steam rising from the locomotives.

*'I'll get them to delay the train for Rouen half an hour.
The light will be better then.'*

'You're mad' said Renoir'

Monet went to see the director of the Western Railway and explained that he wanted to paint either the Gare du Nord or Gare Saint-Lazare but *'...yours had more character.'* The overawed director consented, instructing the engine driver to make steam while Monet sat and painted. Renoir finished the story by saying *'I wouldn't have dared to paint even in front of the corner grocer.'*

THE LIFE OF MONET

~1914~
Eldest son Jean dies
It is suggested that Monet paint a large Water Lily Mural for the French State. France enters First World War on 3 August

~1915~
Monet builds a new studio over 23 metres long to paint *Water Lily* mural

~1918~
Armistice declared on 11 November. Monet donates 8 paintings to the state, chosen by Prime Minister Clemenceau

~1919~
Monet's great friend, Auguste Renoir, dies

~1920~
Monet is offered membership of the 'Institute de France' which is the highest honour the state can bestow on artists. Monet refuses

~1923~
Regains his eyesight after an operation on cataracts

~1925~
Burns some of his paintings as they do not meet his own high expectations

~1926~
Art dealer Rene Gimpel buys two paintings for 200,000 francs each. Monet dies on 6 December.

WHAT DO THE PAINTINGS SAY?

THE BASIN AT ARGENTEUIL, 1872

Monet chose Argenteuil as his new home, moving to a rented house with his young family. Argenteuil was a small town which lay on the right bank of the Seine just six miles from the main Saint-Lazare railway station in Paris. From the 1850's the impact of the railway line was changing the provincial towns surrounding Paris. It enabled Parisians to make day trips to the rural areas as well as enabling those living in the towns to commute to Paris. The railway also had the effect of stimulating industrial growth away from Paris and factories were beginning to be built in the first stages of urban and suburban sprawl. Monet painted many views of the Seine and countryside surrounding his new home.

This view shows families strolling along the river bank. The broken sunlight falls through the trees creating an ideal subject for Monet's brush – the perfect rural idyll. Monet would spend a very productive and happy six years at his home in Argenteuil.

In 1866 Monet painted a picture of the 19-year-old Camille Doncieux. Camille became Monet's favourite model and also his mistress. Monet's father disapproved and cut off his son's allowance. At the same time Monet suffered the blow of rejection of his big painting *Women in the Garden* by the Salon jury. In addition Camille was pregnant and their son, Jean, was born on 8 August 1867. Fearful of the impending war with Prussia they moved to Trouville on the Normandy coast, and subsequently to London and Holland. During this period Monet's struggle to make pictures which would be accepted by the Salon and to establish his career underwent a change. When Monet returned to Paris after the war his commitment to *en plein air* painting was greater than ever. When Boudin saw the paintings Monet brought back from his travels he commented *'I think he's got all the makings and is going to be the leader of our movement'*.

IMPRESSION, SUNRISE, 1872

By 1872 Monet had become disenchanted with the Salon exhibition and had not entered any paintings for consideration. A group of independent painters including Monet, Renoir, Sisley, Degas, Cezanne, Pissarro and Morisot decided to organize their own exhibiting society. On 23 December 1873 the 'Societe Anonyme Cooperative d'Artistes Peintres, Sculpteurs, Graveurs' was founded. An exhibition was planned for April 1874 to be held in the studios of the photographer Felix Tournachon (known as Nadar) on the Boulevard des Capucines. Monet showed nine pictures, including *Impression, Sunrise*.

THE IMPRESSIONISTS

A review of the exhibition by Louis Leroy in the satirical magazine *Le Charivari* has become famous. He entitled the review 'Exhibition of the Impressionists' and so claimed responsibility for naming the movement *Impressionism*. Leroy wrote the review in the manner of two visitors discussing the exhibition:

'What is this a painting of? Look in the catalogue.'
'Impression, Sunrise.'
'Impression - I knew it. I was just saying to myself, if I'm impressed, there must be an impression in there... and what freedom, what ease in the brushwork! Wallpaper in its embryonic state is more finished than this seascape!'

The painting which caused the sensation was of a sunrise over the sea at Le Havre. It was nothing new for Monet. In this picture as in others he strived to create an impression of a rapidly changing scene as the orange sunlight reflected on the shimmering water.

THE CATHEDRAL REVOLUTION

*P*rofessionals will please excuse me, but I cannot resist the desire to establish myself as an art critic for a day. It's Claude Monet's fault. I entered Durand-Ruel's gallery to take a leisurely look again at the studies of the cathedrals of Rouen, which I had enjoyed seeing at the Giverny studio. And that's how I ended up taking that cathedral with its manifold aspects away with me, without knowing how. I can't get it out of my mind. I'm obsessed with it. I've got to talk about it.

And for better or worse, I will talk.' Georges Clemenceau wrote these words in 1895, eleven years before he was elected Prime Minister of France. Clemenceau's great support for Monet helped consolidate the artist's reputation. In 1907, the year after Clemenceau was elected, the state bought one of the Rouen Cathedral paintings for the home of government in Paris, the Palais de Luxembourg.

ROUEN CATHEDRAL, PORTAL, MORNING SUN, HARMONY IN BLUE

In February 1892 Monet rented a room opposite Rouen cathedral. After painting the view of the cathedral several times he changed rooms so as to shift his angle of view slightly. After painting this new view he moved again, and again after more pictures. In all he appears to have changed his viewing angle five times, searching for new highlights and shadows as the sunlight fell across the front of the building. In the three paintings illustrated here Monet explores the effect of light at different times of day and in different weather conditions.

Rouen Cathedral

ROUEN CATHEDRAL, PORTAL, FULL SUNLIGHT, HARMONY IN BLUE AND GOLD

The early morning cool blues observed in the first painting, *Morning Sun. Harmony in Blue* give way in this painting to the warm golds of the full mid-day sun. The early morning mist has cleared to reveal the front of the cathedral. The deep shadows throw the building into sharp relief. Monet painted 31 pictures of the facade of Rouen cathedral. When he exhibited them at Durand-Ruel's gallery in 1895, priced at 12,000 francs, they were a great success.

ROUEN CATHEDRAL, PORTAL, GREY WEATHER, HARMONY IN GREY

In this third picture Monet explores the same subject in overcast weather. There is no direct sunlight and therefore no deep shadow, instead the cathedral stone is much flatter and more evenly coloured. The aims Monet had for his earlier series of paintings on grain stacks are the same as the aims for the cathedral series:

'I'm plugging away at a series of different effects but the sun goes down so quickly at this time of year that I can't keep up with it... the more I do, the more I see what a lot of work it takes to render what I am looking for, instantaneity, above all the enveloppe, the same light diffused everywhere'.

HOW WERE THEY MADE?

In 1839 Michel Chevreul, a Director of Dyeing at the Gobelins tapestry workshop, formulated his law of simultaneous contrast of colours. This stated something that artists had known for centuries but had never been scientifically expressed: colours placed next to each other had an effect on how each was perceived. When complementary colours are contrasted the effect is most intense. For example, a red next to its complementary colour, green, makes the red appear redder; similarly the green will appear greener.

The other fundamental complementary colours are orange and blue and violet and yellow. Monet used this effect to its full in his painting. He said *'... colour owes its brightness to force of contrast... primary colours look brightest when they are brought into contrast with their complementaries'*. Nowhere is this demonstrated better than in Monet's famous painting *Impression, Sunrise detail (above)*.

The range of colours employed by artists today has hardly changed from those being used in the 1870's. The development of new colour pigments and stable chemical compounds was the result of new developments in the expanding industries of France and Germany. The new colours were chiefly developed for the painting, decorating and coach-building trades, but the artist's merchants benefited from the same discoveries. Impressionists such as Monet made full use of these colours. The invention of the collapsible tin paint tube in 1841 by the American painter John Rand had expanded the market for pre-ground colours available over the counter. By the 1870's it was commonplace for artists to get their paints in tin tubes from a widening selection of colour pigments. Some artists still preferred to grind the pigment themselves, mixing the powders into paste with the addition of poppy oils, but most were content to do away with this chore.

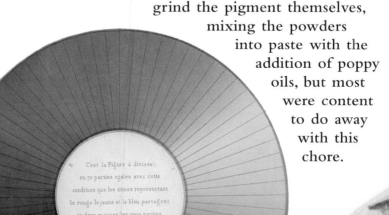

Cest la Figure & divisée en 72 parties egales avec cette condition que les zones representant le rouge le jaune et le bleu partagent en deux moities les trois parties où elles se trouvent.

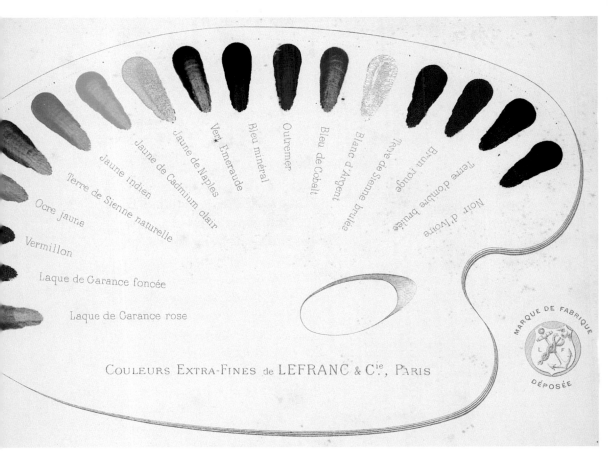

Vermillon

Ocre jaune

Terre de Sienne naturelle

Jaune indien

Jaune de Cadmium clair

Jaune de Naples

Vert Émeraude

Bleu minéral

Outremer

Bleu de Cobalt

Blanc d'Argent

Terre de Sienne brûlée

Brun rouge

Terre d'ombre brûlée

Noir d'Ivoire

Laque de Garance foncée

Laque de Garance rose

COULEURS EXTRA-FINES de LEFRANC & Cᵢₑ, PARIS

MARQUE DE FABRIQUE
L F
DÉPOSÉE

SAMPLE OF LEFRANC & COMPANY'S OIL PAINTS

The Impressionists embraced the new colours that were becoming available. Their obsession with capturing the changing effects of light upon their *motif* meant that they welcomed any scientific advances that could help them in their work. Lefranc sold paint to both the retail and wholesale trades, offering colours ground and unground, mixed with oils for artists. Lefranc even sold empty tin tubes, and pliers to close the tubes. Monet is known to have had colours specially hand ground for him by the colour merchant Mulard in the rue Pigalle.

PORTABLE OIL PAINTS

The collapsible tube was made initially from lead or tin but it was found that lead reacted with chemicals in some paints so tin became the preferred material. The invention of the tube freed the artist from the studio as never before. Because paints suddenly became easily transportable artists were able to work out of doors. Another benefit was that the life of the paint was extended. The previous method of storing paint was to keep it in a small sack (made from pig's bladder) which the artist would puncture with a tack, squeezing out the paint when required; but the paint would harden quickly.

ILLUSTRATED

Paris Fashions
— The Very Latest —

3 d.

FRESH AIR IS
FASHIONABLE

THE ARTIST'S VISION
MONET'S METHODS

The Impressionists made *plein air* or open-air painting famous but there was a tradition of painting out of doors in the nineteenth century. Monet's commitment to it was such that he even dug a trench into which a large canvas could be lowered in order to work on the top portion of the picture without having to change his viewpoint. He worked directly on the canvas, without the normal preparatory drawings, and would be careful to wear dark clothing in order not to reflect light onto the canvas. The sunshade was essential. Without shade the artist would not be able to get the right colours or tones in the glare of the sun. There were other problems. Berthe Morisot complained that... *'the moment I set up my easel more than fifty boys and girls were swarming about me...this ended in a pitched battle...'.*

DETAIL OF WHITE DRESS

THE EVIDENCE

A magnified view of the painting, revealing sand stuck to the surface, is testimony to the *plein air* nature of its execution.

Impressionism is well known for an effect known as the *tache,* which is a coloured stroke or 'patch'. This was an artistic development thought to have been made more widespread in the nineteenth century by the introduction of the flat, square brush as opposed to the round brush. It can be seen quite clearly here in this detail.

flat ferrule brush

THE BEACH AT TROUVILLE, 1870

The scene Monet depicts probably shows Camille, seated on the left wearing a flowered hat, with Madame Boudin in the dark dress. This was painted shortly after Monet's and Camille's marriage on 28 June 1870 as it is known that they stayed at Trouville during the summer. Their son, Jean, was three years old at the time and it could be his shoe that Monet shows casually hanging on the back of the chair. When Monet painted *The Beach at Trouville* he was preoccupied with the effects of changing light. The problems this presented could not have been greater than on the coast with sand reflecting the glare of the sun and very little in the way of shade. It was painted on the beach, and would have taken less than half an hour if we are to believe his statement that...'*no painter could paint more than one half hour on any outdoor effect and keep the picture true to nature...*' although it is possible he returned to the same canvas later.

He had a grooved box built to take wet canvases so he could put one away and take out another, working on several at a time. In order to capture the fleeting effect of the light Monet had to work fast. '*The first painting should cover as much of the canvas as possible, no matter how roughly, so as to determine at the outset the tonality of the whole.*'

FAMOUS IMAGES

*M*any of Monet's paintings are familiar to us today because we are used to seeing them reproduced so many times in books and for other purposes. Impressionist paintings are probably the most popular of all; it is an easily understood art which does not ask the viewer to work hard to understand the imagery. Impressionist painting is 'comfortable' to look at, its summer scenes and bright colours appealing to the eye. It is important to remember, however, that this new way of painting was challenging to its public not only in the way that it was made but also in what it showed. They had never seen such 'informal' paintings before. The edge of the canvas cut off the scene in an arbitrary way, as if snapped with a camera. The subject matter included intimate domestic scenes; pictures of alcoholics; pictures of prostitutes. Never before had these subjects been considered fit for artists. When Monet set about making his paintings he was venturing into unknown territory.

LA RUE MONTORGEUIL ON 30 JUNE 1878

In 1877 Monet had moved back to Paris, staying at an apartment on the Rue d'Edinbourgh. It was here that Michel, Monet's second son, was born on 17 March 1878. On 30 June 1878 a public holiday was declared for the World's Fair. The festival was a big occasion with Parisian streets decorated with flags. Monet made two street paintings. He later said *'On 30 June, the first national holiday, I went out with my painting equipment to Rue Montorgeuil; the street was decked out with flags and the crowd was going wild. I noticed a balcony and I went up and asked permission to paint, which was granted. I came down again incognito'.*

THE POPPY FIELD AT ARGENTEUIL, 1873

Painted in 1873 when he was living in Argenteuil with Camille and son Jean, this picture represents one of the happiest periods in Monet's life. The picture shows two pairs of figures, both comprising a woman and child. It is likely that one couple is Camille and Jean, who would have been five years old when the picture was made. Monet was relatively secure financially although not well off. The previous year had been a success with the Parisian art dealer Paul Durand-Ruel purchasing many paintings. This in addition to his father's inheritance made it possible for them to rent in this rural suburb of Paris. The idyllic scene is at the heart of the appeal of Impressionist painting; a warm sunlit summer's day in a field populated with brilliant red poppies. Monet demonstrates awareness of the contrast of colours effect, placing the dabs of red in a ground of green.

WOMEN IN THE GARDEN, 1866

Edouard Manet's painting *Dejeuner sur l'Herbe* when first exhibited to the public in 1863 caused a scandal. Monet was inspired by this work and in 1865 planned a painting on the same subject but this time to be a truthful depiction of modern life, rejecting references to art history (Manet's painting was full of art historical references) and painted with natural light *en plein air*. The picture would be huge, including twelve life size figures, and would take the 1866 Salon by storm. The picture was never finished, was partially destroyed and cut up into sections which were displayed as paintings in their own right. In 1866 Monet embarked upon an even more daring painting – *Women in the Garden*. For this picture he made no preparatory sketches. Monet worked directly on a canvas two and a half by over two metres in size, working out of doors. It was for this picture that Monet dug a trench, lowering the painting rather than changing his own viewpoint on the subject so concerned was he to recreate exactly what he saw. Eventually Monet conceded defeat and finished the canvas in his studio.

THE LAST OBSESSION

*T*he water lily paintings are often considered by art historians to be the greatest paintings of Monet's career. In 1883 he rented a house at Giverny, fifty miles from Paris. Seven years later he purchased the house and shortly afterwards in 1893 purchased a meadow near the property which contained a pond fed by the Ru River, a tributary of the Seine. He employed at least six gardeners who gradually shaped the meadow into a garden of willows, irises and water lilies specially imported from Japan. Monet painted the gardens around the house and then concentrated on the water gardens, painting them repeatedly between 1897 and his death in 1926.

MONET PAINTING WATER LILIES

This photograph shows Monet in his studio. He is holding a palette and is standing in front of one of his vast water lily canvases. In later years Monet depended more and more on his daughter-in-law Blanche who became his continual companion. Her support was important during this time when he was diagnosed as having cataracts and was frightened of going blind. Monet finally had an operation in 1923 after losing all sight in his right eye. Monet had a large studio built in his garden, measuring 12 by 24 metres, enabling him to paint his huge water lily canvases.

MORNING WITH WEEPING WILLOWS, 1916-26

The vast canvases that Monet painted towards the end of his life are considered today to be important works in the development of modern art. *Morning with Weeping Willows* is made up of three sections (the complete middle section and part of each end panel are shown here – the whole painting is shown on page 31), each measuring approximately 2 by 4 metres. The paintings represent not just what was in front of Monet's eyes but equally a summary of his sensations. Monet was releasing himself from the representation of a scene in order to synthesize the recollections, impressions and sensations that it generated. The 'abstract' qualities of colour and shape were the dominant consideration. Monet emphasised this by combining into a single painting panels of different views that had been painted at different times in different conditions of light. Monet said of these pictures *'I waited for the idea to take shape, for the groupings and composition of themes to slowly sort themselves out in my brain'*. *Morning with Weeping Willows*, part of a donation to the French state at the end of the First World War, was finally unveiled at the Orangerie in Paris in May 1927 five months after Monet's death.

THE WATER LILY POND, HARMONY IN GREEN, 1899

Monet had an arched wooden bridge built across the narrowest part of the pond. He also had to control the flow of the Ru River to raise the temperature of the water in order that the imported water lilies might thrive. This caused the locals of Giverny to protest. The River Ru was used by the local population for their washing and they thought that Monet's 'Japanese Garden' would pollute their water. In 1901 Monet admitted *'These landscapes of water and reflections have become an obsession'*. A gardener was employed to maintain the water lilies in such a way as to suit Monet's paintings.

THE AUDIENCE FOR THE PICTURES

THE DRAMATIST LOUIS FRANCOIS NICOLAIE

This caricature was drawn by the eighteen-year-old Monet.

*M*onet's first sales were of his caricatures. His talent for caricaturing those around him started at school with sketches of his teachers. Monet said of caricature '*... I quickly developed a skill for it. At the age of fifteen, I was known all over Le Havre as a caricaturist... I charged for my portraits at 10 or 20 francs per head... had I carried on I would have been a millionaire by now'*. His earliest serious patron was shipowner Gaudibert when Monet was in his early twenties. Some patrons, such as the department store owner Ernest Hoschede, gave invaluable financial support but the most important figure to support Monet and the Impressionist painters was art dealer Paul Durand-Ruel. Durand-Ruel bought their paintings from the early 1870's and was responsible for showing Impressionism to an international audience in galleries in London and New York. The American patrons became very important to the commercial success of Impressionism. As the paintings became known so American critics and artists followed the fortunes of artists working in France such as Monet.

IMPRESSING AMERICA

In 1870 Monet was staying in London. It was here that he was introduced to Paul Durand-Ruel who had moved his gallery temporarily to London because of the Franco-Prussian war. Monet recalled that '*... without Durand we would have starved like all Impressionists. We owe him everything... he risked everything more than once to support us'*. In 1886 Durand-Ruel organised an exhibition of Impressionist art at the American Art Association in New York. This included 49 works by Monet and was a great success. The following year more Monet paintings were exhibited at the National Academy of Design in New York and the Royal Society of British Artists in London.

April 12th, 1893.

M. A. Ryerson Esq.,
to
Messrs. Durand-Ruel.
----

41 - "L'Ile de la Grande Jatte"	- $300.	
41 - "Place de la Concorde"	- 300.	
39 - "Le Pont d'Austerlitz"	- 350.	
940 - "Pont de Notre Dame"	- 300.	
434 - "La Seine à St. Mammès"	- 350.	
917 - "Aprèsmidi de Septembre"	- 450.	
976 - "Meules, effet de neige"	- 1,500.	$3,550.

Messrs. Durand-Ruel
to
M. A. Ryerson Esq.

	-	$ 450.
No.3366 -	-	= $3,100.

Balance in favor of Messrs. Durand-Ruel

was shipped besides.

SALES RECEIPT FOR IMPRESSIONIST PAINTINGS

This receipt dated 12 April 1893 itemises paintings purchased by the wealthy American collector Martin Ryerson from Paul Durand-Ruel's New York office. It includes the picture *Meules, Effet de Neige* by Monet as well as works by Lepine and Sisley. The success of Impressionism in America helped Durand-Ruel establish his New York office on prestigious 5th Avenue.

A PHOTOGRAPH OF CLAUDE MONET, TAKEN AROUND 1904

GRAIN STACK, SNOW EFFECT, OVERCAST WEATHER

This painting is from the series of fifteen paintings produced by Monet in 1890 and 1891 which explored the same subject time and again in different light conditions. The French title, *Meule, Effet de Neige, Temps Couvert* can be seen on the Durand-Ruel receipt with some variation.

MARTIN RYERSON WITH CLAUDE MONET

This photograph shows Ryerson with Monet in the garden at Giverny. Ryerson was an important collector of art who later became a founding trustee of the Art Institute of Chicago. Partly because of Ryerson's interest the Art Institute of Chicago now holds one of the most important collections of Impressionist paintings in the world.

CAMILLE, OR WOMAN IN THE GREEN DRESS, 1866

In 1865 Monet painted several pictures featuring the young model Camille Doncieux. One picture, called *Camille*, or the *Woman in the Green Dress*, attracted a great deal of attention at the Salon where it was hung. Emile Zola published an article in the daily newspaper *L'Evenement* entitled 'The Realists at the Salon'. It read *'I confess the painting that held my attention the longest is* Camille *by M. Monet. Here was a lively energetic canvas. I had just finished wandering through those cold and empty rooms, sick and tired of not finding any new talent, when I spotted this young woman, her long dress trailing behind, plunging into a wall as if there were a hole there. You cannot imagine what a relief it is to admire a little, when you're sick of splitting your sides with laughter and shrugging your shoulders'.*

WHAT THE CRITICS SAY

The eighth and last Impressionist exhibition took place in 1886. Monet could not be persuaded to take part in this show because of the differences that had grown between him and some of his fellow artists. Degas, always quick to argue, criticised Monet's work as superficially decorative. Degas exhibited 15 pastel pictures of women bathing at the final Impressionist exhibition which was dominated stylistically by Pointillist works such as those of Seurat and Signac. These 'neo-impressionistic' paintings based on scientific colour principles found no sympathy with Monet who turned his back on the new developments to concentrate on his own individual style. In the early days of Impressionism it was the establishment in the form of the official *Salon* and public opinion which had criticised Monet's work. By 1886 his painting was becoming a critical and commercial success and Monet found that the new 'establishment' of the Impressionist exhibitions were being challenged by the scientific objectivity of the Pointillists and the aim of Cezanne *'... to make something solid of Impressionism'.* Art historians have over the course of the last 100 years weighed the relative merits of the Impressionists, neo-Impressionists and those that followed such as Cezanne. As critical fashions change so Monet's work becomes sometimes more, sometimes less, important and influential than those around him.

THE MASTERPIECE

The writer Emile Zola had been very supportive of the new art of Impressionism. In 1886 however he published a book entitled *L'Oeuvre* (The Masterpiece) which casts its leading character, artist Claude Lantier, as a failed dreamer. Several of Zola's friends thought the fictional Lantier was based upon themselves, particularly Cezanne who had until that point been a good friend of Zola. Monet wrote to fellow artist Pissarro *'Have you read Zola's book? I am afraid it will do us a lot of harm'*.

SUNDAY AFTERNOON ON THE ISLAND OF LA GRANDE JATTE

Georges Seurat

This Seurat painting, exhibited at the final Impressionism show of 1886, is typical of the Pointillist style that challenged Monet's Impressionism. Under the influence of colour theorists such as Chevreul (see pages 12 and 13) the Pointillists applied dots of colour scientifically in order that colours are mixed in the viewer's eye rather than actually on the canvas.

CAMILLE, OR THE CAVERN

car caturist Bertall

This caricature was drawn by Charles d'Arnoux who published under the pseudonym Bertall. It was published in the weekly satirical magazine *Le Journal Amusant*. Paintings hanging in the Salon exhibition were ruthlessly caricatured for the amusement of the French public regardless of the fame of the artist. The title for this caricature refers to the dark background against which the figure of Camille is depicted.

IMPROVISATION 28

Wassily Kandinsky

Kandinsky is regarded as one of the founders of abstract painting, painting 'pure' abstract pictures as early as 1910. Kandinsky saw one of Monet's *Grain Stack* paintings (see pages 26/27) in an exhibition in Moscow in 1895 and commented: *'Suddenly, for the first time, I saw a picture. I only learned that it was a grain stack from the catalogue. I couldn't recognize it myself... I vaguely realized that the object was missing from the picture... it had a power I had never even suspected'.*

ART NEWS

Art News was a highly influential journal (an early copy shown left) when the famous critic and art historian Clement Greenberg wrote an article about Monet entitled *'Claude Monet: The Late Monet'* in 1957. In this critical assessment of Monet's work some thirty-one years after the painter's death Greenberg concludes that Monet's vast *Water Lilies* paintings belonged more to *'our time and the future'*. The changing fashions of art criticism are evident from Greenberg's *'dismissal of van Gogh as a great artist, but Monet's example serves better... to remind us that van Gogh may not have been a master'*. In the end it does not really matter what the critics and historians say. Judge the work as it should be judged, with your own eyes.

A LASTING IMPRESSION

Impressionism set out to achieve greater naturalism by trying to capture the effects of light and in doing so challenged the accepted conventions of the day. It not only became the leading artistic movement of its time but a commercial success as wealthy American industrialists with a taste for art became avid collectors of Monet and others. The influence of Impressionism on the succeeding generations of artists was profound, enabling them to push conventional representative art to its limits and beyond into the abstraction which dominated the twentieth century. Today Impressionism is more popular than ever, presenting as it does an enticing world apparently full of warm sunlit landscapes peopled by figures for whom it always appears to be a slow Sunday afternoon. Impressionist pictures are reproduced all around us; on the wall calendar; on greetings cards. It is however important to remember that this was a new art, a shocking art to its public who were unused to the subject matter and the way in which it was depicted.

ENCHANTED FOREST

Jackson Pollock

Greenberg writes: '... *those huge close-ups which are the last* water lilies *say - to and with the radical Abstract Expressionists - that a lot of physical space is needed to develop adequately a strong pictorial idea that does not involve an illusion of deep space. The broad, daubed scribble in which the* water lilies *are executed says that the surface of a painting must breathe, but that its breath is to be made of the texture and body of canvas and paint, not of disembodied colour'*. The paintings of the Abstract Expressionist artist Jackson Pollock owed much to the last great water lily paintings. Both the Monet and the Pollock paintings are about the artist's feelings towards colours, space and pattern across a huge canvas.

GLOSSARY

Abstract - Abstract art is based upon the idea that elements of a picture, such as colour, shape and form, have an intrinsic visual value aside from their use by artists to represent a recognizable subject.

Canvas - Artists usually painted on linen canvas, although cotton and hemp were also available. In Monet's day the canvas could be bought in standard sizes, stretched around a wooden frame and primed ready for use.

Caricature - Normally means a picture of a person, usually a drawing, but can also mean a written or acted representation. The caricature exaggerates characteristic features for comic effect.

Composition - This word is often used as a general term meaning 'painting', however the specific meaning refers to the combination of elements in a picture which the artist strives to bring together to give its an overall visual impact.

Pigment - This generally refers to a powder that is mixed with a liquid to make paint. The powder, usually made by grinding specific minerals or plants, is added to oils for oil painting but can be mixed with other mediums for different types of painting such as fresco or watercolour.

Tonality - Tonality refers to the gradations between light and dark regardless of the colour. A black and white photograph will depend entirely upon tonality to depict the subject, ranging from the brightest white to the darkest black. It is complicated by the fact that artists have to translate tonality into colour.

ACKNOWLEDGEMENTS

We would like to thank: Graham Rich, Tracey Pennington, and Peter Done for their assistance. Copyright © 2004 *ticktock* Entertainment Ltd. First published in Great Britain by *ticktock* Publishing Ltd., Unit 2, Orchard Business Centre, North farm Road, Tunbridge Wells, Kent TN2 3XF.

Printed in China.

Picture Credits t=top, b=bottom, c=centre, l=left, r=right, OFC=outside front cover, IFC=inside front cover, IBC=inside back cover, OBC=outside back cover.

The Advertising Archive Ltd; 2tl. Photo © AKG London; 2cr. Art Institute of Chicago; 27tl, 27br. Art Institute of Chicago/Bridgeman Art Library, London; 29t. © Bibliothèque Nationale of France, Paris; 4tl, 18cb. By permission of The British Library (7857dd,Opp80); 19t. Courtauld Institute Galleries, London. Photo © AKG London; 6/7cb. *Enchanted Forest*, 1947, Jackson Pollock © ARS, NY and DACS, London 1997 (Peggy Guggenheim Collection, Venice. Photo © AKG London); 31br. *Improvisation 28* (Second Version), 1912, Wassily Kandinsky © ADAGP, Paris and DACS, London 1997 (Solomon R. Guggenheim, Museum, New York/Bridgeman Art Library, London); 30tr. Kunsthalle, Bremen/Lauros-Giraudon/Bridgeman Art Library, London; 28tl. Mary Evans Picture Library; 3tl, 3b, 10tl, 16bl, OBC & 20tl, 24bl, 26bl, OBC & 27tr. Metropolitan Museum of Art, New York/Bridgeman Art Library, London; IFC/1 & 5tl & 8tl. Musee d'Art et d'Histoire, St. Denis, Paris/Giraudon/Bridgeman Art Library, London; 2bl. Musee du Louvre. Photo © AKG London; 4b. Musee d'Orsay, Paris. Photo © AKG London; 9tl, 12/13ct. Musee d'Orsay, Paris. Photo © AKG London/Erich Lessing; 6cl, 7tr, OBC & 9br, 10bl, OBC & 10br, OBC & 11cb & 32, 14tl, 16t, 17t, 22bl, 23bl, 25bl. Musee d'Orsay, Paris, France/Giraudon/Bridgeman Art Library, London; 17b, 22/23ct. Musee de l'Orangerie, Paris/Lauros-Giraudon/Bridgeman Art Library, London; 24/25t & 30b. Musee Marmottan, Paris. Photo © AKG London; OFCr & 15t. Musee Marmottan/Giraudon; 26tl. Reproduced by courtesy of the Trustees, The National Gallery, London; 20cl. National Gallery, London/Bridgeman Art Library, London; OFCl & 21t. National Gallery of Art, Washington. Photo © AKG London; 12br. National Gallery of Scotland, Edinburgh/Bridgeman Art Library, London; 27cl & 30cr. Ny Carlsberg Glyptothek, Copenhagen. Photo © AKG London/Erich Lessing; OBC & 11tl. Phillips Collection, Washington DC/Bridgeman Art Library, London; 6tr. The Pierpoint Morgan Library/Art Resource, NY (S0109859); 28/29cb. Private Collection/Bridgeman Art Library, London; 8br. Pushkin Museum, Moscow/Bridgeman Art Library, London; 5cr. Roger Viollet/Frank Spooner Pictures; 5bl. Tate Gallery Archive; 30cl.

Every effort has been made to trace the copyright holders and we apologise in advance for any unintentional omissions. We would be pleased to insert the appropriate acknowledgement in any subsequent edition of this publication.

A CIP catalogue record for this book is available from the British Library. ISBN 1 86007 485 5